CUTE & EASY **Xmas** *Cake Toppers!* CAKE TOPPERS

Cute & Easy Christmas Cake Toppers!
Fondant Fun for any Festive Celebration!

Contributors

Lesley Grainger has been imaginative since birth and has baked since she was old enough to hold a spatula. When life-saving surgery prompted a radical rethink, Lesley left a successful corporate career to pursue her passion for cake making. Lesley is based in Greenock, Scotland. Say 'hello' at:
www.lesleybakescakes.co.uk

Lesley Grainger

Following a career in finance, Amanda Mumbray launched her cake business in 2010 and has gone from strength to strength, delighting customers with her unique bespoke creations and winning several Gold medals at various International Cake Shows. Amanda's **Clever Little Cupcake** company is based near Manchester, UK:
www.cleverlittlecupcake.co.uk

Amanda Mumbray

First published in 2014 by Kyle Craig Publishing

Text and illustration copyright © 2014 Kyle Craig Publishing

Editor: Alison McNicol

Design and illustration: Julie Anson

ISBN: 978-1-908707-60-4

A CIP record for this book is available from the British Library.

A Kyle Craig Publication

www.kyle-craig.com

Contents

Welcome!

Welcome to **'Xmas Cake Toppers'**, the latest title in the **Cute & Easy Cake Toppers** Collection.

Each book in the series focuses on a specific theme, and this book contains a gorgeous selection of beautiful cake toppers perfect for any festive celebration!

Whether you're an absolute beginner or an accomplished cake decorator, these projects are suitable for all skill levels, and we're sure that you will have as much fun making them as we did!

Enjoy!

Fondant/Sugarpaste/Gumpaste

Fondant/Sugarpaste – Ready-made fondant, also called ready to roll icing, is widely available in a selection of fantastic colours. Most regular cake decorators find it cheaper to buy a larger quantity in white and mix their own colours using colouring pastes or gels. Fondant is used to cover entire cakes, and as a base to make modelling paste for modelling and figures (see below).

Modelling Paste – Used throughout this book. Firm but pliable and dries faster and harder than fondant/sugarpaste. When making models, fondant can be too soft so we add CMC/Tylose powder to thicken it.

Florist Paste/Gumpaste – The large and small shoes in this book are made using florist paste as it is more pliable than fondant, but dries very quickly and becomes quite hard, so it is widely used for items like flowers that are delicate but need to hold their shape when dry.

Florist Paste can be bought ready made, or you can make at home by adding Gum-Tex/Gum Tragacanth to regular fondant.

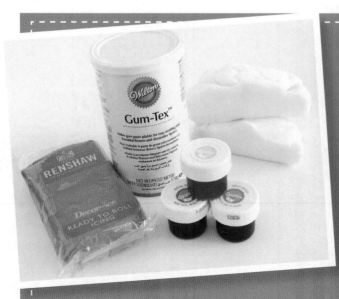

How to Make Modelling Paste

Throughout this book we refer to 'paste', meaning modelling paste. You can convert regular shop-bought fondant into modelling paste by adding CMC/Tylose powder, which is a thickening agent.

Add approx 1 tsp of CMC/Tylose powder to 225g (8oz) of fondant/sugarpaste. Knead well and leave in an airtight freezer bag for a couple of hours.

Add too much and it will crack. If this happens, add in a little shortening (white vegetable fat) to make it pliable again.

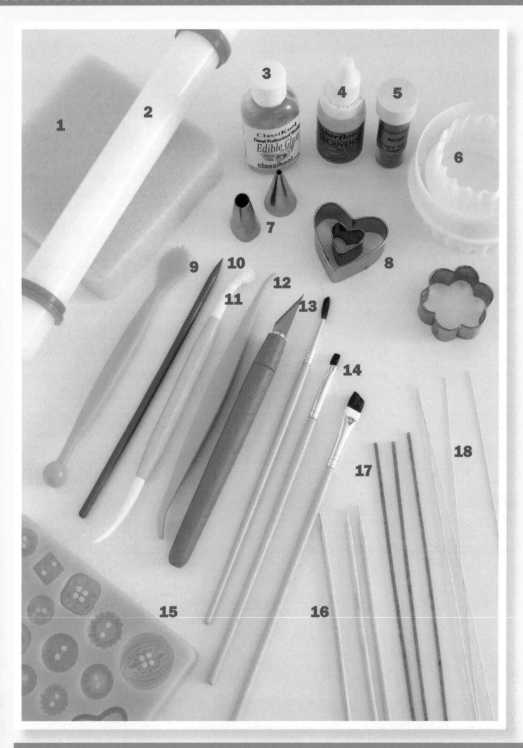

1 Foam Pad – holds pieces in place while drying.

2 Rolling pin – acrylic works better than wooden when working with fondant/paste.

3 Edible glue – essential when creating models. See below.

4 Rejuvenator spirit – mix with food colourings to create an edible paint.

5 Petal Dust, pink – for adding a 'blush' effect to cheeks.

6 Round and scalloped cutters – a modelling essential.

7 Piping nozzles – used to shape mouths and indents.

8 Shaped cutters – various uses.

9 Ball tool/serrated tool – another modelling essential.

10 Small pointed tool – used to create details like nostrils and holes.

11 Quilting tool – creates a stitched effect.

12 Veining tool – for adding details to flowers and models.

13 Craft knife/scalpel – everyday essential.

14 Brushes – to add finer details to faces.

15 Moulds – create detailed paste buttons, fairy wings and lots more.

16 Wooden skewers – to support larger models.

17 Spaghetti strands – also used for support.

18 Coated craft wire – often used in flower making.

Edible Glue

Whenever we refer to 'glue' in this book, we of course mean 'edible glue'. You can buy bottles of edible glue, which is strong and great for holding larger models together. You can also use a light brushing of water, some royal icing, or make your own edible glue by dissolving ¼ teaspoon tylose powder in 2 tablespoons warm water. Leave until dissolved and stir until smooth. This will keep for up to a week in the refrigerator.

Making Faces

The faces featured in this book vary in terms of detail and difficulty. If you're a complete beginner, you may opt to use simple shapes and edible pens to draw on simple features. As your confidence grows, you can use fondant for eyes and pupils, edible paint for features, or combine these methods for some great detailing.

A veining tool will create indents for features.

Pink petal dust adds blush to cheeks.

A mixture of fondant and edible pen can create eyes and eyes and features.

Edible pens can be used to draw on simple features.

Contrasting paste creates a cute muzzle.

Black fondant with white fondant or non-pareils make detailed eyes.

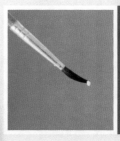
When adding tiny pieces of fondant for eyes, use a moist fine brush.

Cupcake Toppers

When making small figures for cupcakes, it's great to place each on a topper disc, and place this on top of a lovely swirl of buttercream. This way the figure can be removed and kept, and the child can tuck into the main cupcake.

Regular round cutters are essentials, and there are also a great selection of embossing tools and sheets out there that, when pressed into your rolled paste, will create cool quilting effects on your disc. Make your discs first and allow them to harden before you fix your figures to them.

Some figures may use a toothpick or skewer for support, so be sure to take care with these around small children.

Plunger cutters are a great way to add cute details to your models. They cut and then 'push' each small piece out, making it easy to cut small flowers, leaves and shapes.

Painting Details

Many of the projects in this book have beautiful details painted onto the mini items. Mixing regular gel or paste food colouring, or lustre dusts, with rejuvenator spirit will create edible paint in any colour you need. Keep a small collection of fine paintbrushes handy too!

Coloured details – mix your regular food colouring with rejuvenator spirit to create edible paint.

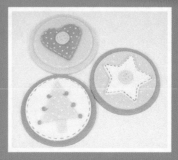

White paint – Americolor Bright White gel paste colour is strong enough to paint on clear white details.

1 Let's start with a comfy chair for our sleepy Father Christmas!

2 Cut two neat blocks of paste and stack as shown.

3 With a sharp knife, cut away the seat section from the middle, and cut down the arms of the chair on each side.

4 Cover the whole piece in a layer of paste, marking the details on with a veining tool. Make a soft square for the seat cushion.

5 Arrange on to an iced cake board, and paint on the holly detail using a fine paintbrush and food colouring mixed with rejuvenator spirit.

6 For his body and legs, roll a long sausage of red paste, tapering at one end for the legs, and a little at the other end for the neck.

7 Make a slit up the longer tapered end to split for legs, and manipulate the paste into the pose shown. Use the veining tool and stitching wheel to mark on some detail.

8 Cut and detail a small triangle of paste to make the flap of his long johns. Make five small white, flat buttons. Insert a skewer ready to take the head.

9 Roll a large ball of flesh paste for his head and insert over the skewer.

10 Roll and flatten some paste for a cushion. Pinch out each corner, and use the serrated end of the cone tool to make the pattern in the centre.

11 Make two teardrop shapes, flatten, and cut away a very small section to make the hand shape. Mark on the fingers with a veining tool.

12 Roll out two tapered sausages for the arms, indenting at the end so you can insert the hands. Arrange the arms over his tummy.

13 Cut a piece of paste for his hair, and mark with a veining tool for extra detail.

14 Cut a piece of paste for his beard, again marking with a veining tool to add texture.

15 Roll two flattened teardrop shapes for the moustache. Mark hair detail with veining tool. Add pink nose and dust cheeks with a little petal dust.

16 Paint or draw on the facial details – sleeping eyes and mouth.

17 Now for Mrs Claus!

18 Roll out a large cone for the bottom of her skirt. Insert a bamboo skewer to support the whole model.

19 Roll out a smaller cone for the upper body and insert over the skewer.

20 Cut out an apron shape, and make the bottom edge wavy. Prick the detail with a toothpick.

21 Cut out a thin strip and attach all the way around the middle.

22 Add a large ball of flesh paste for the head.

23 Add a little nose and two indented ears. Make the arms as before, but just use small balls for her hands. Arrange them as shown.

24 Cut a piece of paste for the hair, adding extra detail with a veining tool.

25 Add a ball of paste to make the bun, marking with a veining tool.

26 Add a fine strip of paste to cover the join.

27 Add a little blossom for some extra detail.

28 Paint or draw on her facial details and dust her cheeks with the pink petal dust.

29 Add some cute details to her outfit by painting some polka dots and some snowflakes.

30 Now let's make an Xmas tree to complete the scene.

 **31** Roll out a large cone of green paste.

 **32** Using a small pair of scissors, snip into the cone.

 **33** Snip all the way up the tree until completely covered.

 **34** Roll out a tapered cone for the base, flattening it at the bottom.

 **35** Add a little strip of paste around the top.

 **36** Insert a bamboo skewer. Leave both sections to dry for a day to firm up, or they will keep toppling over.

 **37** Once semi dried, insert the tree on to the skewer.

 **38** Add a little star to the top.

 **39** Add lots of little differently coloured balls.

 **40** Add the finished tree to the scene.

 **41** Now there's just something missing here – presents for Mrs Claus!

 **42** Make a cube out of some paste – you can make several different sizes.

 **43** Add two strips for the ribbon.

 **44** Cut out a rectangle of paste, and make little cuts all the way along, being careful not to cut all the way across.

 **45** Moisten one of the long edges, and fold the other on top, being careful not to crush the loops that are created.

 **46** Roll the long edge up to create the bow, and glue on top of the present.

Busy Elf

1 Our busy elf needs a cute sleigh to get around in. Let's make one for him!

2 Roll some modelling paste fairly thickly and use the template from the rear of this book as a guide to cut around.

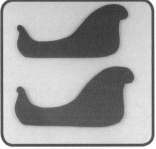

3 Cut out two identical pieces and set aside to dry for 24 hours.

4 Shape a piece of paste into a rectangle about half the length of the sleigh sides.

5 Place the rectangle on to a thick piece of white paste that is the same length as bottom of sleigh sides.

6 Glue the dried sides to cover the red rectangle, leaving the white paste exposed.

7 Cut out two runner shapes, using the templates provided, with a craft knife and leave to dry until firm.

8 Attach the runners to the side of the sleigh.

9 Roll out a long thin sausage of paste and use it to create a fancy design on the sides, gluing in place.

10 Paint the runners and side design with the gold lustre dust.

11 Our elf has a little reindeer friend!

12 Roll out some paste and shape in to a tear drop shape. Insert a toothpick ready for the head.

13 Cut a teardrop shape and glue to the front of the body.

14 Roll out two teardrop shapes for legs, and flatten at the larger ends.

15 Attach the legs to the body, gluing towards the back.

16 Make two smaller tapered sausages for the front legs and glue in place. Add two paler circles to the end of other legs.

17 Roll out a ball of paste for the head, tapering slightly at the top.

18 Cut out a muzzle and glue to the lower half of the head.

19 Make ears from balls of darker and paler paste, flattened together. Attach to the head and make two holes with the end of a paintbrush for the antlers.

20 Roll out a tapered sausage, make a few cuts along it, and soften the cuts by rolling them gently between your fingers. Leave to dry.

21 Once dried, insert the antlers in to the holes on the top of the head.

22 Roll out a ball of red paste for the nose.

23 Paint or draw on the facial details and dust the cheeks with a little petal dust.

24 Now for Mr Elf himself!

25 Roll out a teardrop shape for the body.

26 Cut a circle to make the breeches, and attach to the bottom half of the teardrop shape.

27 Make two holes with the end of a paintbrush, and insert two sausages for the legs.

28 Cut two long strips to make the straps.

29 Cut out two circles for the buttons. Use a smaller circle cutter to make an impression, and prick two button holes with a toothpick.

30 Roll out two teardrop shapes for the feet, and turn up the end of the shoes.

 **31** Sit the elf in the sleigh and push a skewer all the way through him into the sleigh to secure him.

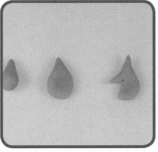 **32** Roll out a teardrop shape, flatten it and cut away a small section for the hands/mittens.

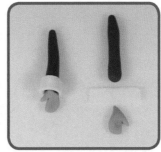 **33** Roll out a tapered sausage for the arms, and a strip for the cuffs. Assemble all the pieces.

 **34** Attach the arms to the body, and cut out a snowflake for the collar.

 **35** Roll a large ball of flesh paste for the head.

 **36** Attach a small ball for the nose, and two pointed teardrop shapes for the ears.

 **37** Cut a piece for the hair, mark with veining tool, and paint on the facial details, brushing the cheeks with a little petal dust.

 **38** Add a tapered cone for the hat.

 **39** Roll out a sausage to make the fur around the hat.

 **40** You may also wish to add some details to your cake.

 **41** Roll out a sausage of green paste and attach to the front of the cake.

 **42** Cut out two strips of paste, and cut V's in the end of each one. Attach to the top of the ring shape.

 **43** Make a little bow using the mould, and attach to the wreath.

 **44** Cut out lots of holly shapes using the cutter and glue them to the ring, covering it completely.

 **45** Roll tiny pieces of red paste to make the berries.

 **46** Make the gifts in the same way as in the previous Mr & Mrs Claus tutorial.

Polar Bears

1 For the sitting figure, roll an egg shape of white paste and insert a toothpick for support.

2 Create two tapered sausages to make the bottom legs and use your veining tool to make 'toe' indentations.

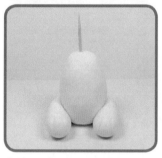

3 Attach to the body, as shown.

4 For the head, roll an egg shape of white paste.

5 Use your fingers to shape the muzzle, as shown.

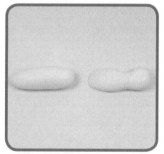

6 For the arms, roll two tapered sausages and pinch gently to create a wrist and paw.

7 Attach one arm only, tilting your figure slightly to the same side.

8 For the scarf, roll a thin, flat strip of coloured paste and use your scalpel tool to create a fringe at each end.

9 Wrap the scarf around the neck area, insert the head onto the skewer, attach the second arm. Create little ears with pads of paste, indented with ball tool.

10 For the laying down bear, roll an egg shape of paste and flatten gently towards the front. Create four legs, as Step 2.

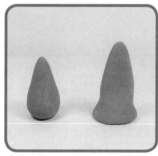

11 For the Santa hat, make a cone of red paste. Gently stretch the base and elongate and flatten towards the top.

12 Add the head (Steps 4 & 5), attach the hat, folding towards the front. Trim the hat with a strip of white paste, a white ball and attach one ear.

13 Add pads of black paste for noses, petal dust to cheeks, paint on eyes and use veining tool to create happy smiles!

14 Use edible white paint to add highlights and details to the noses and scarf.

Christmas Cupcakes

Materials

Modelling paste:
Red, Green
Dark brown, Light brown
Flesh, Black
Orange, White
Yellow, Blue
Petal dust: pink
Edible pen: black
Edible paint: black, red
Rejuvenator spirit
Edible glue

Tools

Craft knife/scalpel
Veining tool
Pastry circles
Bow mould
Holly cutter
Fine paintbrush
Toothpick

1 You will find templates for these cupcake shapes at the rear of the book. First, let's make a santa face cupcake topper!

2 Cut out a hat shape and attach to a disc of flesh coloured paste.

3 Cut a white beard and attach.

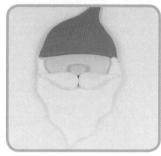

4 Flatten two teardrop shapes for the moustache and add a ball of pink for the nose.

5 Paint in the eyes, dust the cheeks with petal dust, add a strip of white paste for the fur and a flattened ball to the tip of his hat.

6 Now for a cheeky elf!

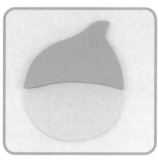

7 Cut a hat shape and attach it to a disc of flesh coloured paste.

8 Add a strip of white for the fur, and a flattened ball of yellow paste to make the bell.

9 Use a small ball of paste for the nose, and make the ears by flattening two teardrops of paste.

10 Paint or draw in the facial and bell details and dust the cheeks with petal dust.

11 Next up, a snowman!

12 Cut a large blue topper circle, then a smaller circle for the head, and the next size up for the body, trimming at the bottom to fit the disc.

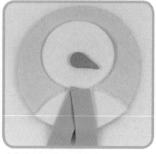

13 Add a flattened teardrop shape for the carrot nose. Cut two strips for the scarf, making cuts at the end for the tassels.

14 Add a piece of paste to cover over the scarf ends and mark with a veining tool.

 **15** Paint or draw on the facial details and dust the cheeks with a little petal dust.

 **16** This little reindeer is too cute to eat!

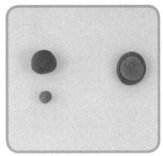 **17** Cute a dark brown topper circle then use the same cutter to make a lighter muzzle section.

 **18** Roll two small balls – dark and light brown - as pictured, and flatten them together to create the ears.

 **19** Attach the ears, and make a red ball for the nose.

 **20** Roll out two tapered sausages, and make cuts along the end to create the antlers.

 **21** Attach the antlers, paint in the facial details and dust the cheeks with a little petal dust.

 **22** A little red Xmas robin!

 **23** Add a small circle of brown paste to a topper disc of paste.

 **24** Add a little red breast to the brown circle, using the same size cutter.

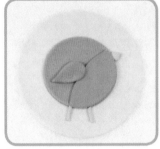 **25** Add two tiny sausages for the legs, a flattened teardrop for the beak, and a second flattened teardrop for the wing.

 **26** Paint on an eye, and dust the cheeks with petal dust.

 **27** Don't forget your Xmas stocking!

 **28** Cut out a sock using the template and glue to a topper disc.

 **29** Add a little strip to the top of the sock, marking it with a veining tool.

 **30** Cut out a tiny circle, and use the same cutter to dissect the circle into two pieces. Arrange them on to the toe and heel.

 **31** Paint on a cute Christmas pattern.

 **32** Yummy – an Xmas pudding on a cupcake!

 **33** Add a little circle of brown paste to a disc.

 **34** Cut out a white circle, the same size as the pudding, and with your craft knife, cut the dripping shape by hand.

 **35** Cut out a piece of holly and attach.

 **36** Roll little tiny red balls for the berries, and paint on some black polka dots.

 **37** Ding dong, it's Christmas time!

 **38** Cut out two bell shapes using the template.

 **39** Arrange the bells onto a disc of sugarpaste, and add little balls to make the clangers.

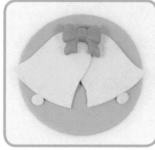 **40** Add a little bow made in the bow mould.

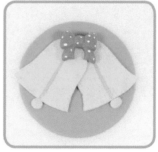 **41** Paint on some cute details.

 **42** A finally, a Christmas gift!

 **43** Add a square to a topper disc of paste.

 **44** Attach strips of paste to make the ribbon.

 **45** Make the loop as shown in the previous Mr & Mrs Claus tutorial.

 **46** Paint on some details to make it look like wrapping paper!

Festive Figures

Materials

Modelling paste:
Red, Green
Flesh, Black
Orange, White
Yellow, Blue
Petal dust: pink
Edible pen: black
Edible paint: black, white
Rejuvenator spirit
Edible glue

Tools

Craft knife/scalpel
Veining tool
Pastry circles
Fine paintbrush
Toothpicks
Gold florist wire

1 If you are placing your models on cupcakes, prepare your fondant covered cupcakes now and set to one side. Now let's make a penguin!

2 Roll out a pear shape for the body, and two little balls for the feet, indenting the toes. Insert a toothpick to support head.

3 Attach a ball for the head.

4 Flatten two teardrop shapes and attach to the side of the body, turning them upwards at the bottom.

5 Roll and cut out contrasting white pieces for the face and chest.

6 Attach a little beak and paint on the facial details, brushing the cheeks with a little petal dust.

7 Add a strip of paste across the top of the head, and two balls of paste to make the ear muffs.

8 Now let's make a cute polar bear!

9 Roll out a pear shape for the body, and insert a tooth-pick to support the head.

10 Roll out two tapered sausages for legs and flatten at the larger end.

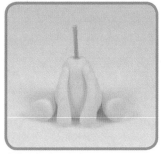

11 Attach these to the body to make the legs, and attach two further tapered sausages for the front legs.

12 Attach a pear shape for the head, shaping the muzzle at the front.

13 To make the ears, flatten two white balls with smaller black balls together and glue to the head. Also attach a black nose.

14 Paint on the facial details, and dust the cheeks with some petal dust. Add two little circles of black to the paws.

15 Shine a light this Christmas with this glowing candle!

16 Roll out a sausage of paste, flattening at both ends.

17 Insert a toothpick.

18 Roll out a teardrop shape, and bend the top over. Attach to the toothpick, leaving a bit of the stick showing, like the wick.

19 Add a flattened teardrop shape in orange to the centre of the flame.

20 Roll out two or three small teardrop shapes, and attach to the side of the candle to look like drips of wax.

21 A heavenly cute angel!

22 Roll out a teardrop shape for the body, inserting a tooth-pick to support the head.

23 Roll a ball of paste for the head.

24 Attach a tiny ball for the nose, and cut out a piece for the hair, marking the detail with a veining tool.

25 Cut out two teardrop shapes for the wings and attach to the angel's back.

26 Paint on the facial detail, and dust the cheeks with petal dust. Twist some gold floristry wire into a halo shape and insert into the top of her head.

27 We definitely cannot forget to make a Santa Claus!

28 Roll out a column of paste and insert a toothpick to support the head. Leave to dry until the column is set solid on the stick.

29 Roll out a ball of paste for the head.

30 Cut out a beard shape and attach to the face.

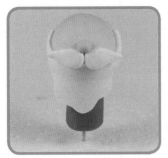 **31** Flatten two teardrop shapes for the moustache and add a pink ball for the nose.

 **32** Add a flattened red ball for the hat.

 **33** Attach a white paste fur trim, and a ball to the top of his hat. Paint on the facial details and dust the cheeks with petal dust.

 **34** Insert the body into the finished cupcake, and add a strip of black for his belt and a square buckle.

 **35** Roll two tapered sausages for the arms, flattened teardrops for the hands, and a strip of white for the fur trim.

 **36** Attach the arms to the body and add buttons, using a toothpick to create button holes. Add a white trim around the edge of the cupcake.

 **37** And now for Mrs Claus!

 **38** Roll a column for her body and insert a toothpick, as in step 28.

 **39** Roll a ball of paste for the head.

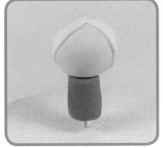 **40** Cut a piece of paste for the hair, marking with a veining tool to add extra detail.

 **41** Add a little nose, and a bun, marking the hair detail on to the bun.

 **42** Add a little strip of paste around the bun, and paint on the facial details, dusting the cheeks with a little petal dust.

 **43** Add a piece for the top half of the apron, pricking it around the edge with a toothpick.

 **44** Insert the body section into an iced cupcake. Cut the apron section, edging with the fluted side of a pastry circle. Prick the edge with a toothpick.

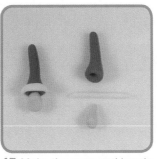 **45** Make the arms and hands as before.

 **46** Attach the arms to the body, and paint some detail onto the skirt.

Robin & Penguin

1 Create a topper disc for each cupcake you are making. Set aside to dry.

2 Roll an egg shaped ball of brown paste to create your robin. Slightly flatten at the base.

3 Shape a flat piece of red paste into an oval shape and attach to the robin's body.

4 To create the Santa hat, roll a pear shape of red paste. Shape by rolling between thumb and forefinger into the shape shown. Glue to the head.

5 Roll a tiny cone of light brown paste and attach as the beak. Cut two small leaf shapes and attach as wings.

6 From black paste, roll two tiny balls for eyes, and cut two little hearts for feet. Attach as shown, adding two white non-pareils to eyes.

7 Add a band of white paste around the hat and fit a 'pom-pom' to the end. Texturise both pieces by pricking gently with a toothpick.

8 For the penguin, create an egg shape from black paste. Shape into an hourglass shape.

9 From white paste, cut a small heart shape and a small circle. Glue both to the body, as shown.

10 Cut a scarf from contrasting paste and drape around the neck, trimming to fit. Use fine scissors to cut fringing detail.

11 From orange paste, cut two small hearts and a tiny square. Fold the square into a beak and glue all in place.

12 Add eyes by rolling two tiny balls of black paste, adding white non-pareils if you wish.

13 Cut a thin strip of grey paste and two pads of contrasting paste to create ear muffs, texturizing as before. Add black 'hair' spikes!

14 Add spotty details using white edible paint.

Materials

Modelling paste:
Brown
Red
Green
White
Black
Non-pareils: white
Edible pen: black
Edible paint: white
Rejuvenator spirit
Edible glue

Tools

Craft knife/scalpel
Veining tool
Pastry circles
Small round cutter
Fine paintbrush
Florist wire
Toothpicks

1 Using your cupcake topper disc for size reference, roll a white egg shape (snowman's body) and a ball (head). Insert a toothpick for support.

2 From black paste, cut a circle and roll a short cylinder shape. Glue together and use your fingers to shape the hat.

3 Roll two small sausages of brown paste around florist wire for support. 'Split' at the end with your scalpel tool, as shown.

4 Roll two thin sausages of red and white paste. Pinch to join them and twist to join together. Roll back and forth to combine them.

5 Roll and flatten two small balls of green paste into a leaf shape and three tiny red balls. Make a small orange nose.

6 Glue all these decorative elements in place. Add little black eyes and 'buttons'. Draw a smile and dust cheeks with petal dust.

7 For the reindeer's body, roll an egg shape from brown paste and insert a toothpick for support.

8 For the legs, roll a slightly tapered sausage then gradually flatten towards the back.

9 Attach the legs to the body and make two gentle notches at the 'feet'.

10 For the head, shape an oval of paste into a bean shape. Roll two tapered sausages for the front legs.

11 Attach the front legs then insert the head onto the toothpick.

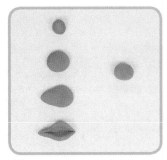

12 For each ear, roll a ball of paste, gently flatten, shape into a flat teardrop then lightly fold, pinching at each end. Roll a little red nose.

13 Create a bow tie with a small rectangle of paste, pinch in the centre then wrap a flat strip over the middle.

14 For the antlers, repeat Step 3. Assemble all pieces together, add eyes and paint on details in white.

Scandi Angels

Materials

Modelling paste:
Black, Flesh
Cream
Light brown
Green
Red
Edible pen: black
Edible paint: red
Rejuvenator spirit
Petal dust: pink
Edible glue

Tools

Craft knife/scalpel
Veining tool
Pastry circles
Heart shaped cutters
Star shaped cutters
Small circle cutters
Small round cutter
Fine paintbrush
Florist wire
Toothpicks

1 Begin by creating cupcake topper discs in the colours of your choice.

2 Create the shape shown (a flat bottomed egg shape!) and insert a toothpick to support the body/head. Allow to dry.

3 Roll a ball of flesh coloured paste for the head and allow to dry. Insert onto toothpick.

4 Cut two heart shapes from thinly rolled paste. Allow to dry.

5 Using edible paint (rejuvenator spirit and food colouring) paint tiny 'stitches' around the edges of the hearts. Allow to dry.

6 Cut a smaller circle of thin light brown paste for hair.

7 Attach to the head, positioning at the fringe. Make a gentle fold at the 'parting'.

8 Continue to attach in gentle folds around the face, gluing as you go.

9 For a halo, take a small length of florist wire, wrap around a small round shape and twist ends together. Wrap with coloured tape (optional).

10 Attach all pieces together. Paint little black dots for eyes and dust cheeks with petal dust to create a rosy glow!

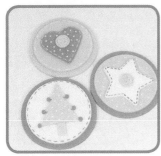

11 Create some pretty co-ordinating cupcake toppers using round cutters, a star cutter and heart cutter. Paint stitches and polka dots galore!

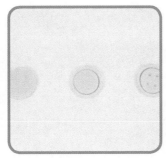

12 To create the buttons, cut little circles of light brown paste, indent gently with a smaller circle cutter and pierce holes with toothpick.

13 To create the Christmas tree cut a triangle of paste to fit your cupcake topper. Cut notches on either side at an angle.

14 You can decorate your little angel with a heart and paint on dots, stitches and stripes.

Gingerbread House

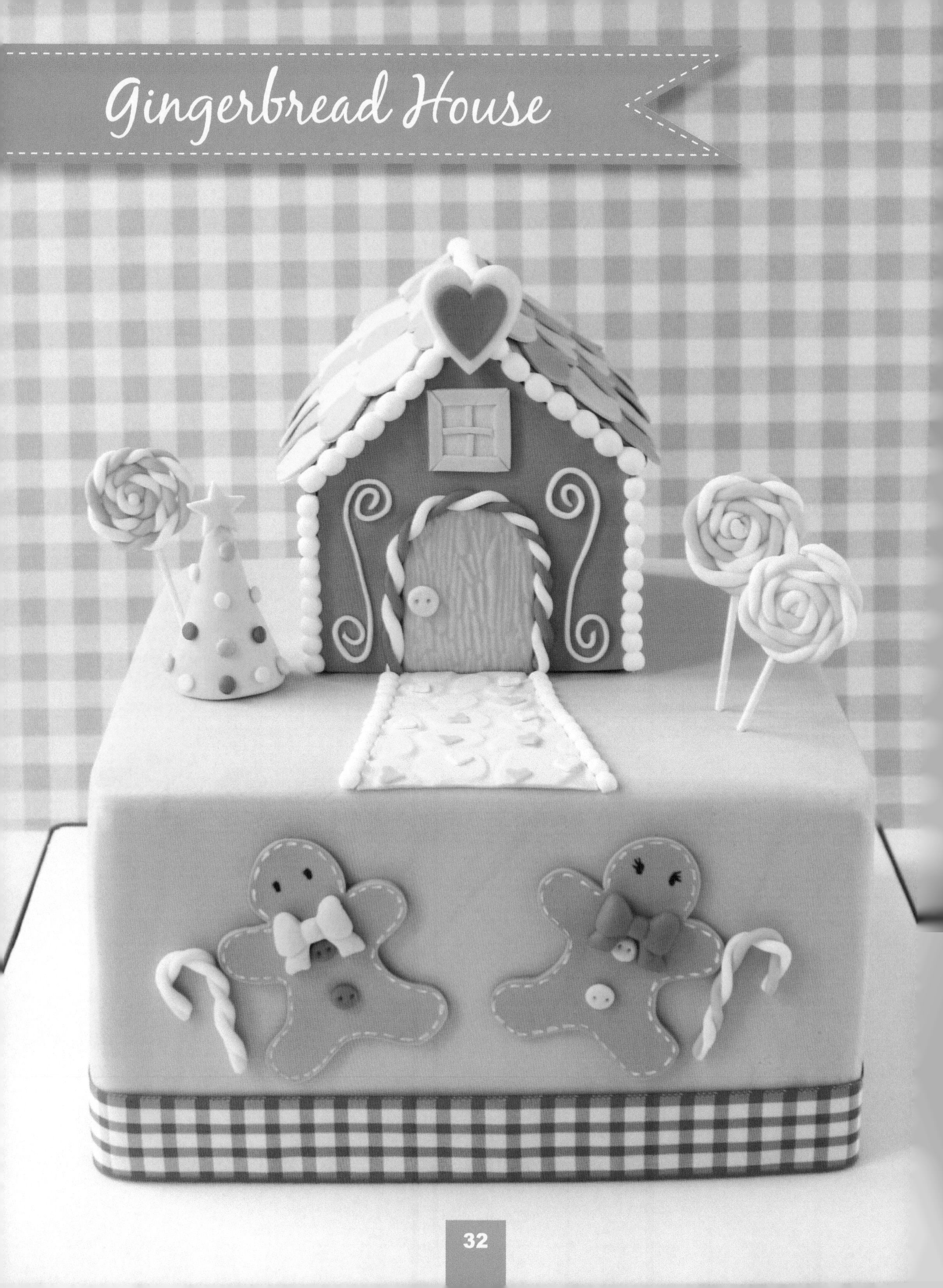

1 Decide on the size of your main cake then make your little house so it fits easily in the centre, with room for the other details.

2 Stack up 10 rice kripsie bars and secure each one to the other with edible glue. Place onto a foam pad as it's much easier to work on.

3 Cut away the top section to make a roof shape.

4 Lean each side onto rolled paste and cut around. Start covering the house with modelling paste, cutting each section with a sharp knife to cut exactly.

5 Continue along each side, leaving the roof exposed for now. Glue each piece in place.

6 Once finished, it should look like this with the roof uncovered.

7 Cut one long piece for the roof. Don't worry about the joins at this stage, and if the roof looks bumpy.

8 Roll lots of white paste balls and glue in place along the roof joins, and across the roof apex.

9 Add slightly smaller balls down the wall edges.

10 Roll out a piece of paste, and then imprint with the woodgrain mat. Cut out a door shape and attach to the front of the house.

11 Roll out two long sausages of paste, one white, one red.

12 Twist the sausages together.

13 Arrange the twisted paste around the door frame. For the handle, cut a small circle, and prick two button holes with a toothpick.

14 Cut out lots of hearts in light and dark brown and leave to dry on a foam pad.

15 Moisten the roof with a little edible glue, and start sticking the hearts to the roof, overlapping them slightly.

16 When you reach the top, cut the pointed end of the heart off before attaching to make it look flush with the white balls.

17 Repeat the process with the other side of the roof.

18 Cut out a small square window and attach to the front of house.

19 Cut out strips to make the window frame, cutting them at an angle to fit together neatly.

20 Attach the frame to the square.

21 Cut out a larger heart and a smaller heart in a contrasting colour. Place the smaller heart in the centre.

22 Glue the heart to the side of the house.

23 Roll out long fine sausages and attach to the sides of the house in a cute design like this.

24 Repeat the design on to the front.

25 Make the heart again as in step 21, and attach to the roof.

26 Imprint some paste with the cobblestone mat, and cut out a path, tapering outwards towards the edge of your cake.

27 Add a row of small white balls at both sides of the path.

28 Cut out some little hearts and sprinkle them on the path, securing with glue.

29 Add in some candy lollipops!

30 Make twists of paste like you did in steps 11 and 12, in three different colours.

 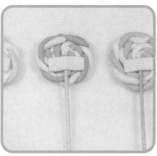  

31 Roll up each twist and secure the ends with a little glue.

32 Flip them over, and glue a toothpick or skewer to the back, and also a little patch of paste to hold the stick in place.

33 Paint the sticks with a little white food colouring and, when dry, insert the lollipops in to the cake.

34 Now to make a little tree.

35 Roll out a cone of paste and attach to the cake.

36 Add a little star to the top.

37 Roll lots of tiny balls in different colours and glue to the tree.

38 You can add some ginger-bread men to the sides of your cake too!

  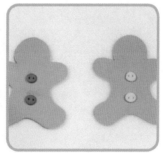 

39 Using the template from the back of this book, cut out the gingerbread men with a scalpel.

40 Cut out two identical shapes.

41 To make the buttons, cut out two circles, and prick in the centre with a toothpick to make the button holes.

42 Make a little bow for each of them.

43 With a fine paintbrush, paint a dotted line around the edge.

44 Paint on some eyes, and dust the cheeks with a little petal dust.

45 Glue both of the ginger-bread men to the front of the cake.

46 Make the candy canes in the same way as in steps 11 and 12, hooking them over at the top and glue in place.

Gingerbread People

Materials

Modelling paste:
Brown
Tan
Red
Green
White
Edible paint: white
Petal dust: pink
Edible glue

Tools

Craft knife/scalpel
Cone tool
Small heart cutter
Fine paintbrush
Toothpicks

1 Prepare a cupcake topper disc for each cupcake you need. We'll start by making the Gingerbread Girl.

2 Create an egg shape for her body, inserting a toothpick to support the head later.

3 For the legs (and arms), roll two tapered sausages. Glue in place, as shown in Step 4.

4 Cut thin strips of white paste and attach in a wavy 'ric rac' style, as shown.

5 For the apron, cut two small rectangles and two long strips of paste for the bib and straps.

6 Use a toothpick to ruffle the skirt, rolling gently back and forth at intervals.

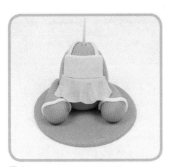

7 Attach your apron pieces, as shown.

8 Attach the arms, adding white wavy trim as before. Add a little heart decoration to apron bib.

9 For her bow, cut a rectangle and a thin strip of paste. Pinch the rectangle in the centre and wrap and glue the thin strip over the middle.

10 Roll a ball of paste for the head. Add two black circles for the eyes and create the mouth with your veining and cone tools.

11 Dust cheeks with petal dust and add details with edible paint. Add a further thin strip of white paste across the head.

12 For our Gingerbread Man, repeat the basic body as before. Create his rolling pin with three little sausages of tan paste.

13 For his hat, make a flat pad of white paste. Make a larger, thicker pad and create 'folds' with your veining tool.

14 Attach all pieces and add detail with edible white paint and petal dust, as before.

More Xmas Cake Topper Ideas!

Why not use some of the skills from previous projects to make these cute & easy festive cake topper ideas?

Festive Faces

Cute Cupcakes

Simple Snowmen

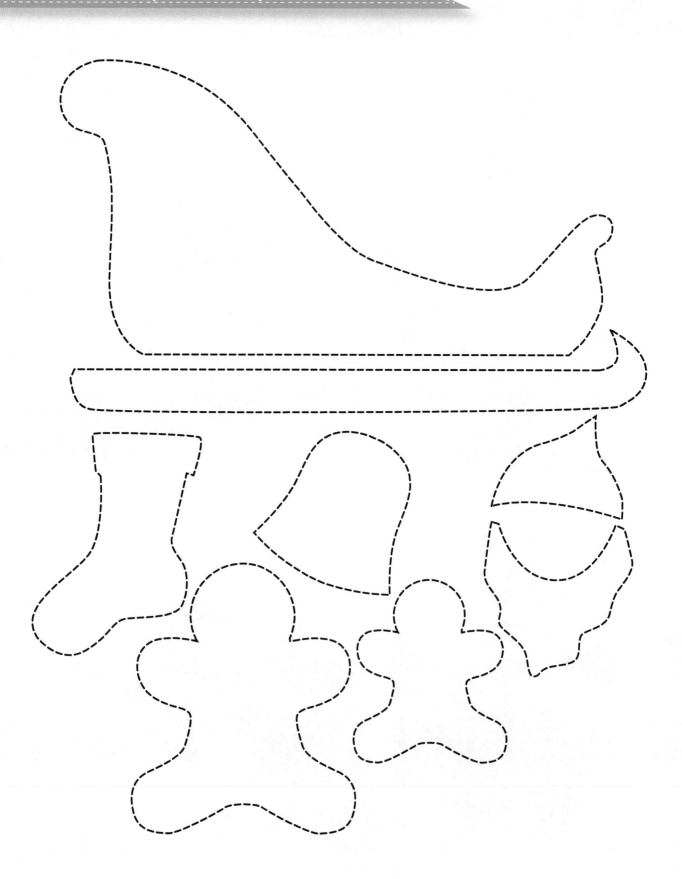

RECIPES ♥ TUTORIALS

Cake & Bake
ACADEMY
Est. 2014

RESOURCES ♥ INSPIRATION

Printed in Great Britain
by Amazon.co.uk, Ltd.,
Marston Gate.